Lucia's

Survival Guide And Cookbook

Lucia's

Survival Guide And Cookbook

Lucille Campilongo

Foreword by Gina Campilongo Friedman

iUniverse Star
New York   Bloomington

Lucia's Survival Guide and Cookbook

iUniverse Star
an iUniverse, Inc. imprint

iUniverse books may be ordered through booksellers or by contacting:

iUniverse
1663 Liberty Drive
Bloomington, IN 47403
www.iuniverse.com
1-800-Authors (1-800-288-4677)

ISBN: 978-1-935278-63-4 (pbk)
ISBN: 978-1-935278-64-1 (ebk)

Library of Congress Control Number: 2009926413

Printed in the United States of America

iUniverse rev. date: 4/29/2009

This book is dedicated to Gina, who was my inspiration for writing this guide.

Contents

Foreword

From Lucia

Before You Eat

Your New Apartment 3

Important Reminders 6

Tips On Cleaning 7

Washing and Ironing 9

Lucia's Really Helpful Hints 12

To Remove Spots and Stains 12

How To Wash Less Frequently 13

Tips On How To Iron 14

Keeping Healthy 16

Now, eat!

My Recipes (the most important part)

Pollo Tegame 20

Breaded Chicken Gina Hates 24

Chicken Cacciatore 26

Whole Roasted Chicken 28

Boneless Breast of Chicken 30

Chicken Soup or Brodo	32
Paella	34
Turkey Breast Cutlets	36
Veal Roast	38
Meatballs	40
Meatloaf	42
Lucia's Version of Joe's Special	44
Sausage and Bean Fry	46
Beef Stew or Veal Sauté	48
Lentil Stew with Spicy Sausage and Cabbage	52
Breaded Veal Cutlets	54
Veal Parmagiano	56
Rice Pilaf	58
Pasta with Butter and Cheese	60
Linguine with White Clam Sauce	62
Linguine with Red Clam Sauce	64
Marinara Sauce	66
Spaghetti Sauce with Mushrooms	68
Putanesca Sauce	70
Pasta with Cucuzza (Zucchini)	72
Pasta with Rosemary and Garlic	74
Mashed Potatoes	76
Fancy Mashed Potatoes	78
Boiled White or Brown Rice	80
Baked Potatoes	82
Roast Potatoes	84
Sautéed Zucchini	86
Boiled Vegetables	88
Breaded Cauliflower	90
Lentil Soup	92
Split Pea Soup	94

Minestrone Soup   96

Beans and Escarole Soup   98

Broth with Cream of Wheat   100

Frittata   102

Frittata with Sausage   104

Nutricious Sample Menus   106

Dessert Anyone?

Forget it! I have writer's cramp—so no more recipes or advice.
I think you can survive for one year on this information.
There are always peanut butter sandwiches, too!

Afterword

About the Author

Foreword

It was the spring of 1980, and although I had been planning for quite some time to spend my junior year of college studying in Italy, the reality suddenly hit my mother like a ton of pizza dough. Her youngest child would be leaving home for almost a year without any knowledge whatsoever of how to cook, clean, grocery shop, or do laundry (but I was pretty smart academically!). Not only would I be leaving home, but I would be living on my own in a foreign country! There were no such things as cell phones or e-mailing. Students generally did not have phone service in their apartments, either. I would be truly on my own in a strange, foreign place. Surely, I was destined to be wearing unclean clothes, living in filth, catching sicknesses, and, worst of all, starving ... heaven forbid!

My mom reacted by switching into emergency mode. I was way too busy to hang around at home getting firsthand instructions from my mom, and she accepted that fact. She had to do something, and that something was to sit down and compose a survival guide that stated matters so simply that even the most domestically challenged would be able to follow it.

The reader will notice that this guide was written by my mom in her speaking style, not in a formal style that one would use when writing for the general public. Also, true to the way Italian families tend to hand down recipes, the reader will notice that amounts of certain ingredients are not always precise. Even for know-nothings like me, the act of cooking must maintain itself as an "art."

My friends and I used to affectionately and humorously call my mom Santa Lucia. She decided to drop the saintly reference and accordingly titled her book *Lucia's Survival Guide and Cookbook*.

It is decades later, and I still refer to her recipes every so often (though I've got the cleaning, laundry, and shopping things down). Faded pages with olive oil stains have started to come loose from their spiral bindings, but the guide remains a vital household force, as my teenagers are starting to learn from it as well.

Lucia's Survival Guide and Cookbook remains a priceless resource for all kids leaving home for the first time, and a good refresher for more seasoned homemakers. Although the world has changed with communication improving and microwave ovens becoming a standard in every kitchen, this guide remains relevant for teaching the basics of cooking and for setting up one's dorm, apartment, or new home. Many of the recipes in this guide are easily adapted for microwave cooking (yes, I've done it). Rest assured, parents, having this guide is the next best thing to you actually being there when they cut the apron strings. After all, I survived …

Gina Campilongo Friedman

From Lucia

On Mother's Day, 2008, my family presented me with a rather unordinary gift. It was a folder filled with unrecognizable papers and e-mail copies. As I read through a few of them, I couldn't quite grasp the meaning of what I was seeing: "congratulations...book published... Publisher's Choice Award..." It took the better part of the day for me to comprehend and, yes, believe that a notebook written by me in 1980 containing recipes and homemaking advice had been published by my children. I was an author! I had forgotten all about the notebook and was unaware that my daughter, Gina (the original recipient of it) was still using the recipes twenty eight years later.

Distant memories came flooding back to me. In the fall of 1980, my nineteen year old daughter would be leaving for Italy. There would be minimal communication between us, and she knew nothing of cooking or practical, everyday domestic matters. How could this have happened? For women of my generation, leaving home without knowing how to cook and clean was almost unheard of.

I remember growing up in the North Beach district of San Francisco, and as a child, would see Italian women (neighbors) exchanging recipes while hanging out the wash. Each province in Italy had its own foods that were indigenous to that region. From many of these women, my mother had learned dishes from northern Italy that were quite diverse from her native Sicilian cuisine. These women took such pride in their homemaking skills. Their wash not only had to be blindingly bright, but shirts hung with shirts, towels with towels, etc. Before they ironed, they checked to see if any of the laundry needed mending. Nothing was left unironed. Permanent press wasn't around when I was a child. Homes in the neighborhood were meticulously clean. God forbid if a bed was left unmade or dishes were left in the sink!

Today they would have been viewed as obsessive, but it was a way of life for these hardworking women and a deep source of pride. Most did not have the advantages of education, so their cooking skills, homemaking and caring for their families became their profession.

That was the world I grew up in, and because of it, raising a family and maintaining a household came almost second nature. By the time my daughters grew up, however, the lives of women had transformed considerably. Women were pursuing college degrees, traveling, playing sports and entering what were formerly inconceivable professions. Homemaking was typically last on a very long list of priorities.

So in 1980 my daughter was leaving for a year in Italy, planning on living in an apartment and she could barely boil water! I was worried. I wrote some basic recipes but didn't stop there. I thought of things she would not know or think about, and started writing in a notebook to make sure she would know what to do if a situation came up. Each time I thought of a problem she might have, I picked up the notebook and wrote like crazy. I didn't know it at the time, but can see now that I was doing this to calm my own anxieties. I wanted to give my daughter a part of me to take with her. All the recipes and advice that I had written down was that "part of me."

Little did I know that nearly thirty years later, my little notebook of worries would evolve into a published survival guide and cookbook. The months following publication were filled with numerous press releases, interviews and even an appearance on the Today show. I still remain flabbergasted by the level of interest that's been generated, but clearly the world has changed, and the skills that my generation took for granted are now considered a diminishing art form.

Another generation has emerged since writing the original survival guide, and now my children have passed the book on to their children. Modern conveniences abound everywhere, and the pace of everyday living seems to always be getting quicker. One thing that hasn't changed, however, is the fact that parents still worry about their children, especially during those transitions into adulthood. Very few parents have the time to actively teach their children domestic skills, let alone write them down. It is my hope that *Lucia's Survival Guide and Cookbook* can help fill the void for all those who might need it, whether they are students, newlyweds, divorcees or anyone who finds themself needing a little help at home.

After each of my recipes, I have included sections for your own notes. Feel free to experiment and adjust my recipes to suit your own personal preferences (I do it all the time!).

Buona fortuna e mangia bene!
(Good luck and eat well!)

Lucia

Before You Eat

Your New Apartment

When you find an apartment, one of the first things to do is go to a supermarket and pick up the following list of staples. I made a list for you so you won't forget the necessary items.

You should always try to have these items in the apartment because even if you can't buy meat, fish, or chicken, you can always turn out a meal with whatever else you have in the house.

With the exception of fruits, vegetables, and dairy products, these staples won't go bad—so always stay well-stocked.

Copy the list when you go shopping for the first time. It will be a lot easier for you.

Staples

Milk

Eggs

Butter

Grated cheese

Hunk of eating cheese (such as Monterey Jack, mozzarella, Fontina, or any other that looks good)

Cottage cheese

Olive oil

Vegetable oil (for cooking)

Wine vinegar

Salt

Pepper

Dried oregano

Dried basil

Dried rosemary leaves

Garlic

Onions

Tomato sauce (six small cans)

Tomato paste (two cans)

Solid pack tomatoes (four large cans)

Cereals Breads

Rice Pasta (for spaghetti)

Pasta (for soup)

Lentils

Dried beans

Canned fruit

Frozen orange juice (if they don't have frozen, get any kind)

Peanut butter

Honey

Tuna (get four to six cans and always keep a few on hand)

Canned soup

Canned broth or consume

Potatoes

Carrots

Celery

Fruit in season

Apples, bananas, and oranges (should always

have them on hand)

Lettuce

Tomatoes

Green onions

Toilet paper (buy a lot; you should never run out of this)

Paper towels

Paper napkins

Plastic wrap (such as Saran Wrap)

Aluminum foil wrap

Dish detergent

Washing detergent

Face soap

Bleaching water (good to use for disinfecting the toilet bowl or cleaning when you first get an apartment)

Cleanser

S.O.S. pads or Brillo pads (good for scrubbing pots and pans)

Rubber gloves

I've listed some brand names but if they don't have these brands, get the equivalent to them!

Important Reminders

Before renting an apartment, check out these things:

1. Do the appliances work?

2. Is there any heat? (remember, winters can be cold)

3. Does the apartment come with dishes, pots, pans, glasses, linens, blankets, pillows, etc.?

4. Is the apartment pretty clean?

5. Are there any signs of mice, roaches, ants, etc.?

6. Is the apartment centrally located? Is it near buses, shopping, and school?

7. Does the landlord seem cooperative, compatible, friendly, and pleasant?

8. And, last but not least, is it in a good neighborhood?

Tips On Cleaning

When you get an apartment, here are the very first things to do:

1. Clean the bathroom. In a bucket, combine some hot water, detergent and a little bleach. Disinfect the toilet bowl and seat (do wear gloves for this).

2. Clean the bathroom and kitchen sinks with cleanser and a little bleach, as well.

3. If there is a drain board area where the kitchen sink is, also wash that well.

4. After this is all done, wash all dishes, silver, pots, pans (scrub pans well with S.O.S.), and glasses.

5. If the inside of the cabinets seem dirty, wipe them out with a rag and some soap or cleanser *before* you put the now clean dishes back.

6. Try to get the kitchen and bathroom very clean before using anything, since this is usually where one picks up germs.

7. Then, move on to the bedroom and check the blankets and linens. If the blankets seem dirty, bring them to the laundromat and wash and dry them. (This is the same for any linens that don't seem clean.) If the blankets are clean but smell musty, hang them out to air for a while. Do the same with the pillows.

8.   Check the closets and make sure that they are clean and dust-free *before* you put your clothes in them.

9.   Check the entire area for bugs and roaches.

10.   Give the apartment a good airing.

If the apartment doesn't supply any cleaning items, you may have to buy:

1.   A mop (for kitchen and bathroom floors) and a bucket. If the bucket is supplied, make sure that it is clean.

2.   Rags.

3.   A dry mop (for hardwood floors).

I'll send you a few dish towels, but you may need more if you are not supplied with any.

Washing and Ironing

By Hand:

- Before washing any clothes by hand, first check the labels for washing instructions. If there are not any instructions, then it is safest to wash the clothes in cold water with a mild soap or detergent (such as Woolite, or anything comparable to it).

- Wash woolens (such as sweaters or anything else that is partially made of wool) in cold water. Let it soak about three to five minutes. Then, rub any spots very gently. Otherwise, do not rub; just squish the woolen around in the water. Squeeze (don't wring or twist) the water out.

Rinse the woolen a couple of times in cold water and squeeze some of the water out. Lay it on a bath towel to dry on a flat surface. When you lay it on the towel, shape the sweater, or whatever you're washing, into the size and shape that it should be. *Don't* pull or stretch.

The woolen may take a couple of days to dry, so if you're planning to wear it the next day after you wash it, forget it! Plan ahead and wash at least three days in advance. When it is almost dry (usually on the second day), hang the woolen on a hanger to finish drying.

- Wash nylons (such as hose, knee-highs, or anything delicate) the same way as you wash woolens, except use lukewarm water. You *do not* have to dry flat. You can dry them on a hanger or over a towel, rack, or clothesline.

By Machine:

- Bring white cottons (such as underwear, towels, dish towels, and sheets) to a laundromat and wash them with regular detergent (use about three-quarters to one cup). Also add one cup of bleach if the load is practically all white, or if nothing can be hurt by bleach.
- Use the delicate cycle on a washer for colored permanent press clothing (usually shirts, blouses and non-denim pants) and for nylon underpants and bras. If it doesn't have a delicate cycle, then put the water temperature on cold or warm, but not hot. Use regular detergent, but *not* bleach!
- When the clothes are finished, put them in the dryer. White cottons can be put on a full cycle in the dryer (usually about thirty minutes). Permanent press clothing should be taken out after ten to fifteen minutes and hung right away on hangers so that they won't wrinkle. Count how many items have to be hung and bring that amount of hangers with you so that you can hang everything right away.

For white cottons, put them into a clean pillow case when they are taken out of the dryer, and then fold them before putting them away.

- Blue jeans and dark socks should be washed together since jeans will throw off some dye when washed. You can put dark brown or maroon things with jeans, along with anything navy-colored. Use cold water and regular detergent, but *not* bleach.

Put them in the dryer for just a few minutes as you do your permanent press. Take the jeans out, hang them, and let them dry naturally for the rest of the time. Otherwise, they will shrink too much. If you have a place outside to hang jeans, do that instead of using the dryer for a few minutes. Socks can be dried for the entire cycle (about twenty-five to thirty minutes).

Of course, the entire wash can always be hung outside to dry if no dryer is available (that is, if it's not raining or too misty). Clothes turn out sunshine fresh!

By the way, a half cup of fabric softener such as Downey or Sta-puf can be added to the last rinse-water. This prevents static cling. See how much scientific stuff I've learned over the years from watching soap operas!

Fabric softener also makes your clothes smell "April fresh" if you can't hang them outside.

Lucia's Really Helpful Hints

When you wash a permanent press garment by hand, hang it up on a hanger and do not wring out any of the water. Hang it dripping wet, and probably just about all of the wrinkles will fall out, and you won't have to iron it.

If you do have to use the iron, you may just have to touch up the items rather than do a full ironing job.

Also, when you hang your things on the hangers, smooth out the fabric and place the items in proper shape while they're still dripping wet.

To Remove Spots and Stains

Blood: Soak the item in cold water and detergent for a while, then rub it with your hands. When the blood is removed, either put the item in the washer with the rest of your clothes, or wash and rinse it by hand.

Grease: While the garment is dry, put some liquid detergent right on the grease spot and let it sit for a few minutes. Then, rub it a little and wash it with your regular wash, or by hand. It's better to try to stay away from greasy things or to wear old clothes before you get close to it.

If you take your clothes to a cleaner and you have some bad spots on them, make sure that you tell the cleaner where the spot came from, such as blood, grease, coffee, etc. If the cleaner knows the source, they can clean it with the proper cleaning solution.

How To Wash Less Frequently

Hang up your clothes the minute you take them off. Do not leave them on the floor or chair.

If the garment seems clean but is wrinkled, chances are that it can be worn again if you iron it just a little.

When you are wearing something that is light in color, try to be careful not to soil it when eating, etc.

Things like underpants, bras, and hose can be washed in the evening when you take them off. Just hang them in the bathroom. Most likely, they will be dry in the morning.

Tips On How To Iron

Blouses or Skirts:

Since these are the items that will have to be ironed the most, please read carefully. First of all, start with the sleeves and …

1. Lay sleeves flat on the table with the seam on one side, and iron both sides of the sleeve.

2. Then, iron the yoke (or shoulders), both front and back.

3. Next, iron the sides, back and front.

4. Finally, iron the collar.

Front

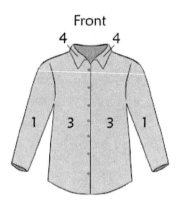

Back

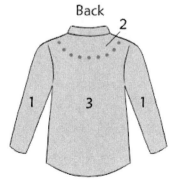

Pants:

Iron the top part of the pants first by slipping the pants onto the table or ironing board. (If I forgot to tell you, be sure to buy an ironing board; ironing on the table is difficult.)

Then, lay the legs flat on the table or ironing board, follow the crease (if there is one), and proceed to iron the leg.

Your pants will stay better if you hang them up, but if you must put them in a drawer, *please* fold them along the crease.

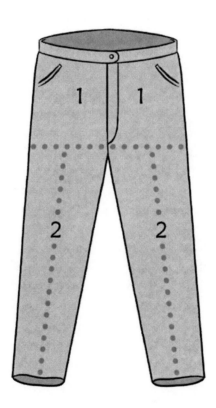

Keeping Healthy

Pretty soon cold and flu season will be coming and, as you know, it's important to stay as healthy as you can so that you don't get behind in your work and activities.

Cold viruses grow in nasal cells and are transmitted from infected people's eyes, noses and hands (where they can live for 2 hours), to surfaces like door knobs (where they can live for days).

A person is most contagious during the first 3 days that they are sick. So, be especially careful during this time. Don't touch your nose or eyes, and wash your hands very often with soap and water. To ensure you do a good job washing, it's been suggested to sing "Happy Birthday" two times while soaping your hands. When you are done singing it twice, your hands should be germ free and ready for rinsing.

If you or someone in your household has a cold, a good thing to do is to use a disinfectant spray (like Lysol). Use it on banisters, toilet handles, faucet handles, light switches, door knobs or any surface that's touched by the person who is sick with any flu or virus.

Remember, besides being clean with things, it's important for your body to be ready to fight any bug. A strong immune system is essential. Eat healthy foods, and drink a lot of water and other liquids. Also rest, get plenty of sleep and find ways to decrease stress. Of course, the old fashioned way now recommended by doctors to fight off a virus, is a nice hot bowl of chicken soup. Heat helps dissolve mucous. Hot tea is also good.

A note concerning allergies: dust mites thrive on sheets, feeding from the skin that you exfoliate. Make sure you wash your sheets and pillow cases in warm water at least every 2 weeks!

Now, eat!

My Recipes

(the most important part)

Some of the recipes that follow, particularly the soups and pasta dishes, were passed on to me from my mother who was from Sicily. Not only are they simple to make and tasty, they also have the added benefit of containing less fat. Since most of these dishes do not contain meat, they tend to also be very economical. Note that with the use of legumes, vegetables, pasta or brown rice, a piece of cheese and some fresh fruit, one can have a complete-protein meal without the fat from meat. In my opinion, this is the true mediterranean diet that physicians often encourage people to follow.

Pollo Tegame

What you need:

~1 fryer (cut up) or 6 chicken breasts or thighs

~oil

~garlic (4 cloves, whole)

~rosemary (dry or fresh)

~salt and pepper

~white wine

~1–2 tbs. of lemon juice, and rind cut into about 6–8 slivers (optional)

What you do:

Wash chicken and dry with paper towels or clean cloth. Sprinkle chicken with salt, pepper, and rosemary on both sides.

Put oil in large frying pan or large pot (enough to cover bottom of pan). Place about four cloves of whole garlic in oil. Heat oil until hot, then put in chicken, skin side down.

Brown the chicken on both sides at about medium-high heat. Take pieces of chicken out of pan and place on a dish if it does not all fit in pan at once. When finished browning chicken, remove just some of the oil (leave a little in the pan and put the discarded oil in a cup or old coffee can).

Now, add enough white wine to the pan so as to cover the entire bottom (about ¼–½ inches high). Stir the wine around with a wooden spoon. Get the brown stuff at the bottom of the pan to mix well with the wine.

Now add all the pieces of chicken (leave the cloves of garlic in), turn heat to simmer, and cover the pan. Let it simmer for about 40 minutes until the chicken seems tender and there is *no* pink when you stick a fork in it.

Turn the chicken once or twice while cooking it. If the liquid dries out too much, add a little water or wine (not too much).

(Optional: You may add some lemon juice and lemon rind slices about 10–15 minutes before chicken is cooked.)

This dish can be prepared ahead of time and then heated before serving. If there are any leftovers, they can be frozen. Place some liquid with the chicken if you are freezing.

Recipe:_____

_____

_____

_____

_____

_____

_____

_____

_____

_____

Recipe:_____

_____

_____

_____

_____

_____

_____

_____

_____

_____

Important Helpful Hints!

Whenever cooking chicken or any other meat that needs to be browned (before you add wine, broth, or tomato paste), you may have to pour out some of the oil from the pan before you add the additional liquid. If the pan contains too much oil, then pour some out so your liquid will not be too oily.

Also, leave the drippings and brown stuff that sticks to the pan and scrape it up with the wine (or other liquid). It makes it taste better and even adds color to the liquid.

When you wash chicken, pull off any excess fat or cut it off (if it will not pull off). Wash it very well and make sure you take off all the coagulated blood and other stuff that doesn't look good.

If you freeze a chicken, wash it before freezing it and pat it dry. Wrap it very well in foil or other freezer paper, and seal it well.

Notes:_____

_____
_____
_____
_____
_____
_____
_____
_____
_____
_____
_____
_____
_____
_____
_____
_____
_____
_____
_____
_____
_____
_____
_____
_____
_____
_____
_____
_____

Breaded Chicken Gina Hates

(But it's really good, and very good to take on a picnic.)

What you need:

~1 cut up fryer, or 6 breasts, 6 thighs, or 8–10 legs

~1 cup (or more) of bread crumbs

~¼ cup of grated cheese

~2 eggs

~oil

~salt and pepper

~garlic powder (optional)

What you do:

Beat eggs with salt and pepper. Put bread crumbs and cheese in another dish and mix together. Dip the chicken in the egg mixture and then in the bread crumbs (coat all over). Put the breaded chicken skin side up in a roasting pan or Pyrex dish (must be oblong-shaped and shallow) with the bottom covered with oil.

Place the pan in a preheated oven at 350 degrees. After about 20–25 minutes, turn the chicken over and cook for the remainder of the time. It should cook a total of 50–60 minutes.

Check with a fork and make sure that no part of it is pink. Take out of the pan and put in a covered bowl after it is fully cooked.

Delicious hot or cold!

🍅 Recipe:_____

_____
_____
_____
_____
_____
_____
_____
_____
_____

🍅 Recipe:_____

_____
_____
_____
_____
_____
_____
_____
_____
_____

Chicken Cacciatore

(a complete meal in one dish)

What you need:

~1 fryer or 6 chicken breasts

~oil

~salt and pepper

~chopped or sliced onions

~1 clove garlic

~2–3 carrots

~2 stalks celery

~2–3 bell peppers

~mushrooms

~1 tomato, tomato sauce, or tomato paste

~white wine

What you do:

Wash and dry the chicken. Put oil in a frying pan or large pot (enough oil to cover the bottom). Sprinkle the chicken with salt and pepper and some oregano. Heat the oil and brown the chicken.

Remove chicken and put on a dish when browned. Then add chopped or sliced onion to oil and 1 clove of mashed garlic. Also add 2–3 sliced carrots, 2 stalks of celery, 2–3 cut-up bell peppers, and sliced mushrooms. Sauté for a while (until onions get sort of limp) then add a cut-up tomato or some tomato sauce or tomato paste (not too much tomato but just enough to color).

Add about ½ cup of white wine. Simmer a few minutes, then put chicken back in the pan. Cover and simmer for about 30–45 minutes.

Excellent with boiled rice or noodles, salad, and French bread.

Recipe:_____

_____

_____

_____

_____

_____

_____

_____

_____

_____

Recipe:_____

_____

_____

_____

_____

_____

_____

_____

_____

Whole Roasted Chicken

(a very easy meat dish)

What you need:

~1 fryer or 1 roasting chicken

~salt and pepper

~garlic powder

~Italian seasoning or rosemary

What you do:

Wash the chicken very well and dry. Then sprinkle the inside cavity of the chicken with salt, pepper, garlic powder, and Italian seasoning (or rosemary). If you can't get garlic powder, put some sliced garlic inside. Sprinkle the outside of the chicken (both sides) with these same ingredients.

Put the chicken in a covered roasting pan that has some oil in it. Place in a preheated oven at 350 degrees for about 1 hour to 1 ¼ hours. Baste once in a while.

Chicken is done when the leg moves easily when you raise it up and down, or when it is easy to puncture the meat between the leg and the breast. If no blood comes out, it is done. Can be eaten hot or cold.

Recipe:_____

_____
_____
_____
_____
_____
_____
_____
_____
_____

Recipe:_____

_____
_____
_____
_____
_____
_____
_____
_____
_____

Boneless Breast of Chicken

(serves 3-4)

What you need:

~4 boneless skinless chicken breast filets

~1–2 eggs, beaten

~bread crumbs

~garlic powder

~butter

~4 green onions

~grated cheese

~salt and pepper

~¼–½ tsp. ginger

~½ can chicken broth, undiluted

~white wine (optional)

~sage (optional)

What you do:

Wash and dry the chicken. Dip in mixture of egg, salt, pepper, garlic powder, and sage (if you decide to use it). Then dip the coated chicken in a mixture of bread-crumbs and grated cheese.

Put cooking oil in frying pan and brown chicken on both sides. Remove chicken and place on a dish.

In a large frying pan with a lid, melt butter and add 4 green onions cut up. Sauté onions until limp. Add ½ can chicken broth. Sprinkle in ginger and add 1 heaping teaspoon of honey. You can also add a little white wine if you like. When sauce bubbles, add chicken and let simmer 15–20 minutes.

Check for readiness by sticking fork in center. If liquid comes out clear, chicken is done. If it comes out pink, chicken needs a few more minutes.

🍅 Recipe:_____

_____

_____

_____

_____

_____

_____

_____

_____

🍅 Recipe:_____

_____

_____

_____

_____

_____

_____

_____

_____

Chicken Soup or Brodo

(good for what ails you or just plain delicious broth)

What you need:

~1 whole chicken

~1 tbs. salt

~4 carrots

~4 stalks of celery

~1 onion

~1 fresh tomato

~parsley (optional)

What You Do:

Wash chicken well and place in large pot. Put enough water in pot to cover chicken. Place on heat (high) and add about one tablespoon of salt. When the water comes to a boil, skim off the foam that comes to the top with a large spoon. Then lower heat and add about 4 carrots and 3 or 4 stalks of celery cut in lengths of about 3 or 4 inches. Also add 1 onion cut into quarters, 1 fresh tomato (cut up in small pieces), and parsley, if you have it.

Let it cook about 1¼ hours to 1½ hours. When cooked, you can take out vegetables and take the amount of broth you are going to use (measure amount with soup dishes). Let the broth come to a boil and add pastina (petite pasta), or you can add cooked rice (cook rice separately, not in broth). You can then eat the chicken and carrots as your entrée with the soup.

This soup is especially good if your stomach is upset or you have a cold, etc. Chicken broth replaces body fluids you lose when you're sick faster than anything. This I read; I'm not making it up!

PS You can also cook tortellini right in the broth after it is made … delicious!

Important: If you don't want to eat chicken with soup for some goofy reason, then turn to the next recipe and see what you can do with it.

🍅 Recipe:_____

_____

_____

_____

_____

_____

_____

_____

_____

_____

🍅 Recipe:_____

_____

_____

_____

_____

_____

_____

_____

_____

_____

Paella

(another meal-in-one)

What you need:

~cooked chicken

~oil

~1 onion

~1 clove of garlic

~1 ½ cup of rice (white rice)

~fresh tomato or tomato sauce

~3 cups of broth

~salt and pepper

~shrimp

~peas (optional)

What you do:

In a frying pan, put enough oil to cover the bottom. Add 1 sliced onion and start sautéing it. When onion is limp, add 1 clove garlic, mashed or chopped. Add 1 ½ cups of raw rice (white rice). When rice starts to get golden, add 1 cup of fresh tomatoes or a little tomato sauce. Then add about 2 to 3 cups of broth (fresh, canned, or consume, etc.). Add enough to cover the rice by about ½ inch. Then add salt and pepper, canned or fresh shrimp (or prawns), and peas (optional). And now here it comes … have chicken all cut up in large chunks (off bone) and add it too. The combination of shrimp and chicken is good. Let mixture cook about 20–25 minutes and serve hot. You can make this with shrimp alone or with fresh clams and chicken. Be creative!

🍅 Recipe:_____

_____

_____

_____

_____

_____

_____

_____

_____

_____

🍅 Recipe:_____

_____

_____

_____

_____

_____

_____

_____

_____

_____

Turkey Breast Cutlets

(serves 3-4)

What you need:

~4 turkey breast cutlets

~1–2 eggs

~bread crumbs

~garlic powder

~grated cheese

~salt and pepper

~choice of chicken broth, consume, or white wine

What you do:

Dip cutlets in mixture of egg, garlic powder, salt, and pepper. Dip cutlets into mixture of bread crumbs and grated cheese.

Fry until golden. Put in preheated 350 degree oven covered by either white wine, chicken broth, or consume, and cook for 10–15 minutes covered.

🍅 Recipe:_____
_____
_____
_____
_____
_____
_____
_____
_____
_____

🍅 Recipe:_____
_____
_____
_____
_____
_____
_____
_____
_____
_____

Veal Roast

(You can cook beef roast the same the way, except 20 minutes for each pound.)

What you need:

~rolled veal roast

~salt and pepper

~garlic powder or two cloves of garlic

~fresh or dried rosemary

~potatoes

~consume (or broth or white wine)

What you do:

Buy a rolled veal roast and sprinkle with salt and pepper generously. If you can get garlic powder (not garlic salt), sprinkle that on your meat, too. Also put some fresh rosemary or dried rosemary all over. If you can't get garlic powder, make several small slits in the meat on both sides and put slices of garlic in slits. Make slits with a sharp pointed knife (just shove knife in with point). Use about 2 cloves of garlic.

Place in 400 degree preheated oven. After about 20– 25 minutes, when meat starts to brown, take pan out (carefully with pot holders) and put meat in a dish. Then drain all oil out of pan and put the meat back on. Add either consume, broth, or white wine, and cook at 325 degrees until done. Baste occasionally! Bake each pound 30 minutes. For example, a 3 lb. roast takes 1 ½ hours to cook. You can add potatoes about 40 minutes before the meal is done.

Recipe:_____

_____

_____

_____

_____

_____

_____

_____

_____

_____

Recipe:_____

_____

_____

_____

_____

_____

_____

_____

_____

_____

Meatballs

What you need:

~2 lbs. of ground beef (or ground veal)

~½ red onion (chopped)

~4 green onions (chopped)

~2 slices of bread (cut up into small pieces and moistened with water)

~¼ cup grated cheese

~salt and pepper

~2 eggs (beaten)

~consume, broth, or spaghetti sauce

~chopped garlic and parsley (optional)

What you do:

Combine all of the ingredients (except the consume, broth, or sauce) together in a bowl. Make sure that all of the ingredients are dispersed fairly evenly throughout the ground meat and not clumped together.

Roll meat between hands into balls and flatten slightly. Fry in preheated oil in a frying pan until they are brown on both sides. Then put in a bowl with a little of either consume, broth, or spaghetti sauce, and heat in preheated oven at 350 degrees for 20–30 minutes.

🍅 Recipe:_____

_____
_____
_____
_____
_____
_____
_____
_____
_____

🍅 Recipe:_____

_____
_____
_____
_____
_____
_____
_____
_____
_____

Meatloaf

What you need:

~2 lbs. ground beef

~¼–⅓ cup chopped onion

~2 slices bread (whole wheat)

~6 oz. chili sauce

~grated cheese

~salt and pepper (to taste)

~1 or 2 eggs

What you do:

Put meat in large bowl. In another small bowl, break up bread in small pieces and add just enough water to wet it. With your hands make bread mushy (if you don't have enough whole wheat, use 3 slices of French bread, or bread crumbs). Add salt, pepper, onions, bread, chili sauce, and cheese to meat. Mix with hands or fork. Add one egg and mix into meat. If meat seems a bit dry, then add another egg.

(Optional: You can add a pinch of oregano, a pinch of thyme, a couple of dashes of Worcestershire sauce, or dash of garlic powder.)

Put in meatloaf pan (loaf pan) or put in roasting pan and shape into loaf. Do not put oil in bottom of pan. Place in preheated 350 degree oven and bake for 1 hour.

If using a metal pan (not a meatloaf pan), you can put a little water on bottom of pan. Don't ever pour water on a Pyrex pan if it's hot, or you'll crack the pan.

If you make this for just the two of you, you'll have another meal from it, or you can make sandwiches the next day.

This recipe serves 4 people generously. You can mix everything together ahead of time, cover, and refrigerate.

Good company dish—easy!

🍅 Recipe:_____

_____

_____

_____

_____

_____

_____

_____

_____

🍅 Recipe:_____

_____

_____

_____

_____

_____

_____

_____

_____

Lucia's Version of Joe's Special

What you need:

~1 lb. ground beef

~1 12 oz. box of frozen spinach

~1 or 2 cloves of garlic chopped

~5 or 6 eggs

~3 tbs. grated parmesan cheese

~salt and pepper to taste

What you do:

Thaw the spinach or immerse it in boiling water until it is no longer frozen. Squeeze water out of spinach. Brown meat in frying pan until it is no longer red. Add the spinach and the garlic to the meat and mix well. Beat 5 or 6 eggs with salt and pepper and grated cheese. Add to the meat and spinach mixture and stir occasionally until eggs have cooked. Taste and add salt and pepper if needed.

🍑 Recipe:_____

_____
_____
_____
_____
_____
_____
_____
_____
_____
_____

🍑 Recipe:_____

_____
_____
_____
_____
_____
_____
_____
_____
_____
_____

Sausage and Bean Fry

What you need:

~3 or 4 large precooked sausages (any kind) sliced into ¼ in. rounds and casing removed

~1 or 2 cans white or kidney beans (drained and rinsed)

~1 onion sliced

~1 or 2 tbs. brown sugar

~2 tbs. ketchup

~1 teaspoon mustard

What you do:

Put just enough oil in a frying pan to lightly coat the bottom (don't put a lot of oil because the sausages throw off fat). Add the onion slices and sauté until onion becomes limp. Add sausage to the pan and mix with the onion. Cook together about 3 minutes. Then add beans, ketchup, brown sugar and mustard. Cook on medium high for an additional 5 minutes or until it's hot.

🍅 Recipe:_____

_____
_____
_____
_____
_____
_____
_____
_____
_____
_____

🍅 Recipe:_____

_____
_____
_____
_____
_____
_____
_____
_____
_____
_____

Beef Stew or Veal Sauté

What you need:

~2 lbs. of beef chunks (or veal)

~4 potatoes

~1 medium-sized onion (chopped)

~4 carrots

~2 stalks of celery

~1 large can of peas

~1 eight-ounce can of tomato sauce

~2 cloves of garlic

~chopped parsley (optional)

~¼ cup red wine (optional)

What you do:

Put oil in a large pot (enough to cover bottom), heat oil, and then put chunks of beef in (if you want you can coat the beef in some flour before you put in oil; the reason you do this is if you want a thicker sauce in the stew). Turn the meat on all sides and when it's browned on all sides, take out of pot. Then add chopped onion in the pot and sauté until a golden color. Add garlic, parsley, and tomato sauce. If you don't have wine, add about ¼ cup of water or any broth. When mixture comes to a boil, add meat, carrots, and parsley that have been cut up. (Carrots are peeled and cut into pieces about 1 inch or more long. Cut washed celery in chunks about ½ inch long). Also add salt and pepper, and you can add a pinch of thyme, basil, or oregano if you want. Turn heat down and cover pot. Simmer for about 1 ½ hours and then in the last ½ hour, add peas. Cook until they are done.

About 45 minutes before stew is cooked, you can add 3 or 4 potatoes cut up into chunks. Then ½ hour after you've added the potatoes, add the peas.

You can also use veal chunks instead of beef; if so, don't cook as long! Just cook it for 1 hour; and don't put peas in. You can put black olives in and use white wine instead of red.

Recipe:_____

_____

_____

_____

_____

_____

_____

_____

_____

Recipe:_____

_____

_____

_____

_____

_____

_____

_____

_____

Important Helpful Hints!

When cooking any stew or sautéed meat, don't cook the meat in tremendous amounts of fluid or sauce.

Use your own discretion. Just put enough sauce or liquid to just cover the meat slightly. In other words, when the meat and vegetables are all in the pot, some of it should be sticking out of the fluid; don't have it all submerged.

Also, don't make sauce too "tomatoey." Keep tomato on the lighter side when you first put it in, then you can always add a little more if necessary.

Notes:_____

_____

_____

_____

_____

_____

_____

_____

_____

_____

_____

_____

_____

_____

_____

_____

_____

_____

_____

_____

_____

_____

_____

_____

_____

_____

_____

_____

_____

Lentil Stew with Spicy Sausage and Cabbage

What you need:

~1 lb. cooked sausage, casings removed and cut into rounds

~3 cups lentils

~2 peeled carrots diced

~1 medium onion chopped

~3 stalks celery diced

~1/2 cabbage sliced ¼ inch thick

~4 cups low salt chicken broth

~1 tbs. olive oil

~salt and pepper to taste

What you do:

Heat oil in a large pot. Then add onion, carrots and celery. Sauté until the onion is limp (about 5 minutes). Add the lentils and broth. Bring to a boil and cook about 15 minutes. Add cabbage and sausage, and return to a simmer. Cover and cook until cabbage and lentils are tender (about 15 or 20 minutes). If the stew seems too thick, add water until you get the consistency that you like. Season with salt and pepper.

This recipe makes quite a lot. If it isn't all eaten, freeze in batches. Defrost overnight in the refrigerator and heat gently.

Recipe:_____

_____
_____
_____
_____
_____
_____
_____
_____
_____

Recipe:_____

_____
_____
_____
_____
_____
_____
_____
_____
_____

Breaded Veal Cutlets

(easy meat dish)

What you need:

~buy veal that's from the leg or any veal that's cut fairly thin (about ¼ to ⅛ inch)

~1–2 eggs

~salt and pepper

~bread crumbs

~grated cheese

~vegetable oil

~white wine or broth

What you do:

Depending on how much veal you are cooking, add 1– 2 eggs. Add salt and pepper. Mix some bread crumbs with a little grated cheese in a separate dish.

Dip the meat in the egg mixture and then in the bread crumb batter. Fry in a frying pan that has vegetable oil lightly covering the bottom. Make sure the oil is hot before you put the meat on it. Cook each side of the meat until golden brown. Cook at medium-high heat.

Can be cooked ahead of time and then warmed in the oven for 15–20 minutes. You can add a little white wine or a little broth if warming in the oven. Cover and heat.

Recipe:_____

_____

_____

_____

_____

_____

_____

_____

_____

_____

Recipe:_____

_____

_____

_____

_____

_____

_____

_____

_____

_____

Veal Parmagiano

What you need:

~veal

~consume

~marinara sauce

~Monterey jack, mozzarella, or Swiss cheese

~chopped parsley

What you do:

Cook veal as you do veal cutlets. When meat is all cooked, take a pan that goes into the oven (rectangular or round) and put a little consume or broth on the bottom (just enough to cover the bottom). Then place the meat on top.

Spoon some marinara sauce over the meat. Put sliced Monterey jack, mozzarella, or Swiss cheese over the meat. Cover the pan with foil and heat in a preheated oven at 350 degrees for 20 minutes or so, until the cheese is melted. You can sprinkle some chopped parsley on top just before serving.

I've included a marinara recipe with the sauce recipes. This dish can also be made ahead of time and is a *great* company dish!

Recipe:_____

_____

_____

_____

_____

_____

_____

_____

_____

_____

Recipe:_____

_____

_____

_____

_____

_____

_____

_____

_____

_____

Rice Pilaf

What you need:

~rice (brown or white)

~4 tbs. butter

~½ medium chopped onion

~chopped parsley

~1 garlic clove

~consume, chicken, or beef broth

What you do:

In a saucepan, put about 4 tbs. butter, add chopped onion (about ½ medium onion), and sauté. When the onion looks transparent, add chopped parsley and 1 whole clove of garlic. Then add 1 cup of uncooked rice (white or brown).

Stir until the rice starts to get a golden color and then add 2 cups of liquid, such as consume or chicken or beef broth. If using canned broth, use the contents of the can plus enough water to equal 2 cups of liquid. Mix all this together. This serves 2–3 people.

Recipe:_____

_____
_____
_____
_____
_____
_____
_____
_____
_____
_____

Recipe:_____

_____
_____
_____
_____
_____
_____
_____
_____
_____
_____

Now... a number of ways to make pasta. Easy!!!

Pasta with Butter and Cheese

(the most basic recipe—and some variations)

What you need:

~any kind of pasta (1 lb. serves 2–3 generously)

~salt and pepper

~pasta

~butter

~grated cheese

~chopped parsley

What you do:

Bring a pot of water to a boil with salt. Put in pasta. Cook until tender or al dente. Drain well. Add some butter (a nice chunk), grated cheese, and pepper. You can also add some chopped parsley to it for color.

This is the basic way to cook pasta. If you use spaghetti sauce, then omit the butter and just add sauce to the drained pasta. Or just add pesto to the pasta instead of sauce.

Or … heat olive oil with 2–3 whole cloves of garlic. When the oil is hot and the garlic is a golden color, take the garlic out and pour the oil over the pasta and add grated cheese.

Recipe:_____

_____

_____

_____

_____

_____

_____

_____

_____

Recipe:_____

_____

_____

_____

_____

_____

_____

_____

_____

Linguine with White Clam Sauce

(easy and a good company dish, too)

What you need:

~1 ½–2 lbs. linguine

~4 tbs. butter

~5–6 green onions

~parsley

~a couple cloves of fresh garlic

~oregano

~2 cans whole baby clams

~white wine

~salt and pepper

~grated Parmesan cheese

What you do:

Put butter in sauce pan. Cut up about 5 or 6 green onions and put in pan. Sauté until onion just barely begins to turn a little golden. Then add a good handful of chopped parsley (preferably fresh parsley). Also add a couple of cloves of chopped or mashed garlic to pan, and a couple of pinches of oregano. Take off heat.

Then when the pasta is cooking, add 2 cans whole baby clams to onion mixture and some white wine (about ¼ cup or little more), and let simmer for a few minutes. Add salt and pepper while simmering. Pour over drained pasta and add grated cheese.

This sauce serves about 4 people and is enough for 1 ½–2 lbs. of pasta. If you want to make it for just two people, use one can of clams and cut down amount of onions to about 4. Serve with a salad.

Recipe:_____

_____

_____

_____

_____

_____

_____

_____

_____

Recipe:_____

_____

_____

_____

_____

_____

_____

_____

_____

Linguine with Red Clam Sauce

What you need:

~1 lb. linguine

~28 oz. solid pack tomatoes (pope or pear variety)

~3–4 green onions

~parsley

~2–3 cloves garlic

~tomato paste (small can)

~oregano

~salt and black or red pepper

~whole baby chowder clams (nt. wt. 10 ¼ oz.)

~red wine (optional)

What you do:

(Have all ingredients cut before browning anything.)

Sauté onion until limp. Add parsley, mashed garlic, and tomatoes. Add a couple of tablespoons of tomato paste and juice. If sauce looks too thick, add a little water. Add salt and pepper (black or red), and sprinkle of oregano.

Simmer ½ hour. Sauce can be prepared ahead of time, but clams cannot be added until 5–10 minutes before serving. Some clam juice or red wine can be added if the sauce isn't too watery.

Toss with cooked linguine.

Recipe:_____

_____

_____

_____

_____

_____

_____

_____

_____

_____

Recipe:_____

_____

_____

_____

_____

_____

_____

_____

_____

_____

Marinara Sauce

(extra easy)

What you need:

~1 lb. pasta (any kind)

~vegetable oil

~4–6 cloves of fresh garlic

~chopped parsley

~2 large cans solid pack tomatoes

~basil

~salt and pepper

What you do:

Put vegetable oil in large pot or large frying pan (enough to cover bottom). Chop or mash 4–6 cloves garlic and put in oil. Also, add a large handful of chopped parsley (fresh preferably). Heat oil and when oil seems hot (do not brown parsley or garlic), add cut up or chopped solid pack tomato (2 large cans). Then add liquid from cans and also some dried or fresh basil, salt, and pepper. Simmer uncovered about 45 minutes to 1 hour (no longer).

This recipe can also be used on veal Parmagiano or eggplant Parmagiana.

Any sauce left over can be frozen or refrigerated, but use in less than a week if refrigerated.

Recipe:_____

_____
_____
_____
_____
_____
_____
_____
_____
_____

Recipe:_____

_____
_____
_____
_____
_____
_____
_____
_____
_____

Spaghetti Sauce with Mushrooms

What you need:

~1 lb. pasta (any kind)

~1 medium sized onion

~1–2 cloves garlic

~parsley

~1 can mushrooms or some dried mushrooms

~3 cans (15 oz.) tomato sauce

~salt and pepper

What you do:

Chop 1 medium onion and put in pan with oil. Sauté onion until golden colored. Add 1–2 cloves chopped or mashed garlic. Also add some chopped parsley, basil (a couple of pinches), and 1 can drained mushrooms or some chopped dried mushrooms.

Sauté few more minutes, then add about 3 cans tomato sauce and about 1 ½ cans of water. Add salt and pepper and bring to boil, then put on simmer and cook for about 1 hour uncovered.

Important: If using dried mushrooms, below is the way to prepare:

Break up into small pieces with your hands before wetting them. Soak in warm water for a few minutes, and rinse in colander several times. Then put in pot with enough water to cover (about 1 or 2 inches higher than mushrooms). Bring to a boil for about 3–5 minutes. Take out of pot with slotted spoon or drain water into a bowl and save water. Add mushrooms to onion mixture and use mushroom water instead of plain water (about 1 ½ cans).

For meat sauce:

Use 1 lb. ground lean beef and brown in pot before you add mushrooms, parsley, and herbs. Crumble meat with spoon and brown completely. Then, add rest of ingredients of the mushroom sauce.

Recipe:_____

_____

_____

_____

_____

_____

_____

_____

_____

Recipe:_____

_____

_____

_____

_____

_____

_____

_____

_____

Putanesca Sauce

What you need:

~1 28 oz. can crushed tomatoes

~1 28oz. can whole tomatoes

~1 15 oz. can tomato sauce

~1/4 cup green olives cut into quarters

~1/4 cup black olives cut into quarters

~1 tbs. capers

~2 shallots chopped

~6 or 7 cloves garlic chopped

~ 3 tbs. fresh parsley

~red pepper flakes

~salt and pepper

What you do:

Sauté the shallots, garlic and parsley until they are soft. Break up whole tomatoes with hands or fork, or put into food processor. Once broken up, combine with the crushed tomatoes and the tomato sauce. Add tomato mixture to the shallots, garlic and parsley. Add a little salt and black pepper and also about 1 cup of water or a little less. Let sauce cook about ½ hour to 45 minutes.

Meanwhile, cut up green olives and black olives. Add olives and capers to the sauce during the last 5 to 10 minutes of cooking. Turn off heat.

Cook any type of pasta (but I wouldn't use cappellini).

This amount of sauce will be enough for 2 lbs. of pasta. If using less, you can freeze half of the sauce. You can cut the recipe in half, but it's best to make the full amount and freeze half of it, so you'll have it for another time.

Recipe:_____

_____

_____

_____

_____

_____

_____

_____

_____

_____

Recipe:_____

_____

_____

_____

_____

_____

_____

_____

_____

_____

Pasta with Cucuzza (Zucchini)

(easy—zucchini can be cooked earlier in the day)

What you need:

~1 lb. pasta (long kind)

~zucchini

~whole cloves garlic

~salt and pepper

~grated Parmesan cheese

What you do:

For 1 lb. of pasta, use about 5 or 6 zucchini. Cut washed zucchini in rounds (fairly thin slices about ¼ inch thick). In frying pan, put in oil and about 4 cloves whole garlic. Heat oil and place zucchini in oil in a single layer. Salt and pepper one side of the zucchini. Turn them over when they are golden and beginning to brown just a tiny bit. Let them turn golden color on other side and then take out of pan and put in bowl. Repeat this until all of them are cooked.

Cook pasta and when pasta is almost done, put zucchini back in frying pan and heat. Drain pasta and then pour zucchini and oil over pasta and mix gently. Put grated cheese on top.

PS When you're through cooking zucchini, don't throw oil away. Turn off heat and save.

Recipe:_____

_____
_____
_____
_____
_____
_____
_____
_____
_____

Recipe:_____

_____
_____
_____
_____
_____
_____
_____
_____
_____

Pasta with Rosemary and Garlic

What you need:

~1 lb. pasta (any kind)

~1 cube butter (8 oz.)

~1 cube bouillon, smashed

~1 pinch rosemary

~4 cloves garlic (mashed)

~½ cup Parmesan

~salt and pepper

What you do:

While pasta is cooking, melt butter on a low flame in a frying pan. In order, add bouillon, garlic, rosemary, salt, and pepper, while stirring continuously. If butter or garlic start to burn, add a small amount of water from the pasta pot.

When pasta is done, combine with everything in the pan and toss. Add ½ cup of Parmesan and toss again.

🍅 Recipe:_____

_____
_____
_____
_____
_____
_____
_____
_____
_____

🍅 Recipe:_____

_____
_____
_____
_____
_____
_____
_____
_____
_____

Mashed Potatoes

(serves 2-3 people)

What you need:

~4–5 large potatoes

~salt

~butter

~milk

What you do:

Peel about 4–5 large potatoes and cut up in chunks. Put in pot with enough water to cover potatoes. Add salt (about 1 teaspoon). Bring to a boil and then reduce heat and cover. Cook about 15–20 minutes (until you can insert a fork in potatoes and the potato seems fairly soft, but not mushy where it dissolves).

Then carefully strain in colander. Put potatoes back in pot or bowl and mash. Add about 2 tablespoons butter while mashing, and then add a little milk. If you want to do it right, add hot milk instead of cold.

If you feel a bit like a gourmet cook and want to be a little fancy, here's what you can do (turn page) …

🍅 Recipe:_____

_____
_____
_____
_____
_____
_____
_____
_____
_____

🍅 Recipe:_____

_____
_____
_____
_____
_____
_____
_____
_____
_____

Fancy Mashed Potatoes

What you need:

~everything from previous mashed potato recipe

~1 green onion

~cheese slices

What you do:

After you've mashed potatoes, take a Pyrex pie plate or small bowl that can be put in oven. Rub some butter on bottom and sides with hands.

Add to potatoes 1 green onion cut up fine, and mix well. Then place potatoes in buttered dish and spread evenly. Slice some cheese and place on top of potatoes. You can use mozzarella, Swiss, cheddar, or any kind. Then place dish in preheated oven 350 degrees for about 20 minutes, until cheese is melted.

This dish can also be made ahead of time and then warmed in oven just before eating.

🍎 Recipe:_____

_____

_____

_____

_____

_____

_____

_____

_____

_____

🍎 Recipe:_____

_____

_____

_____

_____

_____

_____

_____

_____

_____

Boiled White or Brown Rice

(serves 2-3 people)

What you need:

~1 cup rice

~1 tbs. butter

~1 tsp. salt

~grated cheese (optional)

What you do:

Put 2 ½ cups water, butter, and salt in pot. Bring water to boil and then add rice. Turn heat to simmer and cover pot. Cook about 20 minutes until rice is tender (taste it). Rice should have absorbed all of water. If you wish you can add a little more butter and grated cheese.

This is the same recipe for brown rice.

If the recipe is too skimpy for 3 people, then put a little more than 3 cups water and 1 ½ cups rice. Double the recipe for 4 people or more.

🍅 Recipe:_____

_____

_____

_____

_____

_____

_____

_____

_____

_____

🍅 Recipe:_____

_____

_____

_____

_____

_____

_____

_____

_____

_____

Baked Potatoes

What you need:

~potatoes

~salt and pepper

~butter

What you do:

Scrub potatoes with vegetable brush. If you don't have brush, wash well with hands under running water. Cut an X on potato or make a slit in it about 1 inch long (you do this so steam escapes and potatoes won't explode in oven). If you have aluminum foil, wrap in foil. If not, don't sweat it, just put in oven at about 400 degrees for 1 hour or until you can pierce it with a fork easily.

Serve with butter, salt, and pepper. If you can get sour cream, cottage cheese, or yogurt, they also go well with it.

Recipe:_____

_____
_____
_____
_____
_____
_____
_____
_____
_____

Recipe:_____

_____
_____
_____
_____
_____
_____
_____
_____
_____

Roast Potatoes

(serves 3)

What you need:

~4–5 potatoes

~cooking oil

~salt and pepper

What you do:

Peel about 4 or 5 potatoes and put in a bowl or pan of water until ready to cook. The reason you do this is to keep the potatoes from turning brown. Cut potatoes in large chunks. Preheat oven to 350 degrees. Put a little oil in bottom of roasting pan. Dry the potatoes with paper towels or clean dish cloth. Put them in roast pan, sprinkle with salt and pepper, and place in oven. Cook until fork penetrates easily, about 40–45 minutes.

Turn potatoes once after about 20 minutes.

You can add one sliced onion and mix with potatoes before putting in oven, or you can add these potatoes around any roast, such as veal, beef, or lamb.

🍅 Recipe:_____

_____

_____

_____

_____

_____

_____

_____

_____

🍅 Recipe:_____

_____

_____

_____

_____

_____

_____

_____

_____

Sautéed Zucchini

(serves 3 people)

What you need:
~5–6 zucchini

~½ small onion

~butter

~salt and pepper

What you do:

Put some butter in frying pan or large pot and melt (enough butter to cover bottom of pan when melted). Add sliced or chopped onion and brown. Add zucchini chunks or slices and sauté over medium-low heat. Add salt and pepper and cover the last 5 minutes. Don't overcook vegetables.

You can use this recipe for artichokes, bell peppers, peas, and mixed vegetables.

🍅 Recipe:_____
_____
_____
_____
_____
_____
_____
_____
_____
_____

🍅 Recipe:_____
_____
_____
_____
_____
_____
_____
_____
_____
_____

Boiled Vegetables

(vegetables sautéed in garlic)

What you need:

~vegetables

~olive oil or butter

~salt and pepper

~garlic (for sauté)

What you do:

Bring water to a boil and put in cut up vegetables. Lower the heat and cover. Cook until vegetables are tender. Check with fork or taste. When cooked, add salt, pepper, and a little olive oil.

You can use butter instead of oil. This recipe can be also used for almost any vegetable.

To sauté vegetables in garlic, it's best to boil vegetables and strain. Then put in frying pan that has olive oil and a couple of cloves of garlic in it. Heat oil and garlic and then add vegetables to oil, and add salt and pepper. Stir until vegetables are heated and coated with oil.

Recipe:_____

_____
_____
_____
_____
_____
_____
_____
_____
_____

Recipe:_____

_____
_____
_____
_____
_____
_____
_____
_____
_____

Breaded Cauliflower

This is a dish Nonna used to make, which
I loved. She would par-boil the cauliflower,
then bread it and fry it. Being a bit on the
lazy side, I opted for a quicker version.

What you need:

~1 cauliflower (washed and cut up in chunks)

~1 egg

~garlic powder

~salt and pepper

~bread crumbs

~grated cheese

What you do:

Beat egg and add a little salt, pepper, and garlic powder. Dip cauliflower
chunks in egg, then into mixture of bread crumbs and grated cheese.
Put into a pan that has oil in bottom and bake at preheated oven 350–
375 degrees (about 30–40 minutes), turning cauliflower as it turns a
golden color.

Delicious cold too!

🍅 Recipe:_____

_____
_____
_____
_____
_____
_____
_____
_____
_____

🍅 Recipe:_____

_____
_____
_____
_____
_____
_____
_____
_____
_____

Lentil Soup

What you need:

~2 cups lentils

~1 small onion (chopped)

~4 carrots (sliced)

~4 stalks celery (sliced)

~1 can (8 oz.) tomato sauce, 1 cut up fresh tomato, or 2 tbs. tomato paste

~1 clove garlic (chopped or mashed)

~salt and pepper

What you do:

Make sure there aren't rocks or dirt in lentils. To do this, pour a few into palm of your hand and discard any that don't look good or any rocks. Place lentils in colander and pour warm water all over them by placing them under running water and turning them with your hand.

Put enough oil in large pot to cover bottom of pot. Put chopped onion and garlic in and sauté until onion and garlic grow limp. Then add carrots and celery and stir around a few minutes (about 2–3 minutes). Add washed lentils and tomato and mix together with vegetables. Then, add 8–9 cups water. Add about 1 tsp. salt and some pepper. Let soup come to a boil and then put on simmer and cover pot. Let it cook 1–1 ¼ hours. Taste lentils to make sure they are cooked. Also if it needs more salt, add it.

Then, cook some pasta or brown rice (as you cook any pasta or brown rice) and add to lentil soup.

For pasta: Use about 1 cup short pasta (such as shells or the kind you use for macaroni salad).

For rice: Use 1 cup brown rice.

Recipe:_____

_____

_____

_____

_____

_____

_____

_____

_____

_____

Recipe:_____

_____

_____

_____

_____

_____

_____

_____

_____

Split Pea Soup

What you need:

~2 cups split peas

~1 small onion (chopped)

~4 carrots (sliced)

~4 stalks celery (sliced)

~salt and pepper

What you do:

Do everything the same as you do for lentil soup. Wash the split peas (as you did lentils), and add to vegetables, then add water. For split peas, use 8 cups water.

Then when cooked (it takes about the same amount of time to cook), you can also add cooked pasta or white rice.

Recipe:_____

_____

_____

_____

_____

_____

_____

_____

_____

_____

Recipe:_____

_____

_____

_____

_____

_____

_____

_____

_____

Minestrone Soup

(This recipe takes more time, so make it only if you have the time, and *voglia*.)

What you need:

~2 cups dried beans

~1 small onion

~4 carrots (sliced)

~4 stalks celery (sliced)

~1 can (8 oz.) tomato sauce, 1 cut up fresh tomato, or 2 tbs. tomato paste

~½ head of cabbage

~2 zucchini

~1 pk. frozen Swiss chard

~1 pk. frozen peas

~1 pk. string beans

What you do:

You do the same as in lentil soup, except you use dried beans that have soaked in water overnight. Discard the water they were soaking in and add the beans to carrots, celery, and onion mixture. Then add about 12– 14 cups water. Let them cook about 1 hour, then add chopped cabbage, cut up string beans, sliced zucchini, Swiss chard, peas, or whatever vegetable you want. Let simmer until the beans are cooked. It may take another hour or so. This recipe makes a very large pot (enough soup for maybe 3 different times). What you don't use, you can freeze, or cut the recipe in half.

Recipe:_____

_____
_____
_____
_____
_____
_____
_____
_____
_____

Recipe:_____

_____
_____
_____
_____
_____
_____
_____
_____
_____

Beans and Escarole Soup

What you need:

~1 head escarole

~1 can (15 oz.) cannellini beans

~4 cups chicken or beef broth

~1/2 onion chopped

~6 cloves garlic chopped

~1 pinch red pepper flakes

~1 tbs. olive oil

~salt and pepper

~grated parmesan cheese

What you do:

Cut base of the escarole: rinse and drain leaves. Cut leaves crosswise into ¼ inch wide strips.

In a 4 or 5 quart pan, add the oil, onion and garlic. Stir often until the onion is limp (3 to 5 minutes). Add the broth and beans, cover and bring to a boil over high heat. Stir in escarole and cook until it's wilted. Add salt and pepper to taste. Serve in bowls and sprinkle grated cheese on top.

Recipe:_____
_____
_____
_____
_____
_____
_____
_____
_____
_____

Recipe:_____
_____
_____
_____
_____
_____
_____
_____
_____
_____

Broth with Cream of Wheat

(very economical)

What you need:

~1 15 oz. can beef or chicken broth

~3 tbs. 1 Minute Cream of Wheat

~grated cheese

What you do:

Place broth in a pot and let come to a boil. Slowly stir in Cream of Wheat. Lower heat if necessary and continue stirring and cooking for 1 minute. Take off heat and put a lid on the pot. Let it sit for 1 additional minute. Pour into a soup dish and sprinkle with Parmesan cheese or any hard cheese that's grated.

This dish is very nutritious. It's particularly good if you're hungry and want something to eat fast or if you aren't feeling too well and need something that's light and not upsetting to your stomach. Italians have fed babies this for years and have added a beaten egg (stirring it in slowly) while the Cream of Wheat is cooking. You can also use pastina instead of Cream of Wheat with the egg. The broth, egg and pastina dish is called straciatella.

🍅 Recipe:_____

_____

_____

_____

_____

_____

_____

_____

_____

_____

🍅 Recipe:_____

_____

_____

_____

_____

_____

_____

_____

_____

_____

Frittata

(good nutritious dish—*protein!*)

What you need:

~6 zucchini

~1 medium sized onion

~8–9 eggs

~milk (about ½ cup)

~bread crumbs (about 3 tbs.)

~¼ cup grated cheese

~salt and pepper

What you do:

Sauté zucchini in frying pan with onion. When cooked, remove from heat. Put eggs in bowl and add the rest of all ingredients. Beat well with egg beater.

Put just a little oil in an oblong Pyrex dish or any baking pan. Rub oil on bottom with hand and on all the sides of pan. Then, with a ladle, put half of egg mixture on bottom of pan. With a slotted spoon, place vegetable evenly on egg mixture. Then put remaining egg mixture on top of vegetables. Put pan in preheated oven at 350 degrees and cook for about 30 minutes until a golden color. Insert knife blade in center and if knife comes out clean, frittata is done. About 15–20 minutes after you take out of oven, cover it with foil or plastic wrap.

This recipe is a basic recipe and you can substitute any other vegetable, or you can mix, for example, zucchini and bell pepper if you don't have enough zucchini. Artichokes are great too.

Frittata, salad, and some French bread or panini is an excellent meal, and it's excellent when cold too! Good for sandwiches!

Recipe:_____

_____
_____
_____
_____
_____
_____
_____
_____
_____

Recipe:_____

_____
_____
_____
_____
_____
_____
_____
_____
_____

Frittata with Sausage

What you need:

~1 lb. spicy pork sausage

~6 zucchini

~6 bell peppers sliced in strips

~1 medium sized Bermuda onion

~9–12 eggs

~milk (about ½ cup)

~½ cup bread crumbs

~½ cup grated cheese

~salt and pepper

What you do:

Sauté the onion and bell peppers. When the peppers are almost cooked, add the zucchini. Brown the pork sausage in another pan and drain off the fat. Add the sausages to the vegetables after they are cooked.

Beat the eggs, milk, salt and pepper, cheese, and bread crumbs. Pour half of this mixture into a lightly oiled baking dish. Spread the vegetables and sausages evenly on top (pick up with slotted spoon so that you don't get oil into it). Pour the rest of the egg mixture on top and bake at 350 degrees for about ½ hour.

Recipe:_____

_____
_____
_____
_____
_____
_____
_____
_____
_____

Recipe:_____

_____
_____
_____
_____
_____
_____
_____
_____
_____

Nutricious Sample Menus

(Low Calorie, but healthy and will give you energy)

Breakfast: Any 3 or 4 from here:

1. cereal (such as Total, Cheerios, oatmeal and raisin bran)
2. fresh fruit
3. eggs
4. toast
5. juice
6. yogurt

Lunch:

1. salad with chicken and vegetables, tofu or beans
2. turkey or chicken sandwich with cheese, tomato and lettuce or peanut butter with jam or grilled cheese sandwich

Dinner:

1. chicken or any protein (about 4 oz. or about the size of the palm of your hand)
2. vegetables
3. potatoes, couscous, wheat bulgar or pasta
4. vegetable or fruit salad
5. dessert such as fresh fruit, ice cream, cake or cookies

Numbers 1, 2 and 3 are the most important ones to eat every day for dinner. You could substitute, but make sure you get protein, grains, fruits and vegetables daily.

Eat sensibly and I'm sure you will feel good, and when you feel good and have energy, you will do good!

Afterword

Lucia continues to pride herself in the profession and art of homemaking, and she's still cooking! She enjoys experimenting with old and new recipes alike, continually striving for improvements, while introducing new flavors to the family. Her husband, Victor, and her three grown children are always eager recipients of her handiwork.

Since writing this guide, Lucia has been blessed with four grandchildren, all who are now in their teens or young adulthood. Ahhhhhh! More mouths to feed and more kids starting out on their own! Some of the grandchildren have already made Lucia's marinara sauce. The result? They now turn their noses up at the mere suggestion of using jarred pasta sauce. Spoiled kids!!!

About the Author

Lucille Campilongo was born Lucia Burrafato on March 30, 1930 in San Francisco, California. She grew up in the North Beach district of San Francisco which, at the time, was dominated by Italian Americans and Italian immigrants. Central to their culture was, and still is, the importance of food. Not only necessary for mere sustenance, its preparation, and the dining experience that followed, seemed to give the rhythm and the life force that characterized the neighborhood. Even today, it is difficult to think of North Beach without thinking of food.

Lucille learned the arts of cooking and homemaking from her mother. In addition, Italian neighbors often shared their recipes amongst each other. Never afraid of experimentation, Lucille's dishes have elements of almost every region in Italy and some American influences as well.

Lucille currently resides in San Rafael, California with her husband, Victor.

CPSIA information can be obtained at www.ICGtesting.com
Printed in the USA
LVOW041303240812

295686LV00003B/3/P